# THE BEATLES

# RICHARD BRASSEY

Who had 17 number one hits, more than anyone else before or since?

Who once played to a worldwide TV audience of 400 million people?

Whose fans screamed so loud they couldn't hear themselves play?

*The Fab Four! The Lovable Moptops! The Topper–most of the Poppermost!!*

**THE BEATLES !!!**

JOHN LENNON

PAUL McCARTNEY

GEORGE HARRISON

RINGO STARR

All four Beatles were born in Liverpool during the Second World War and grew up and went to school in and around the city.

Ringo was the first to be born. John arrived next, during an air-raid. He was given the middle name Winston after the famous wartime Prime Minister, Winston Churchill. Paul and George came along later, when the worst bombing was over.

John's aunt had to dodge the bombs as she raced to the hospital the night he was born.

Liverpool was a tough place to live during the war. It was often bombed by the Germans. But at last peace returned and with it hope for the future. Even so, times were hard.

When he was five, John's mother and father split up. Neither felt able to look after him so he went to live with his Aunt Mimi. Just down the road was an orphanage in a big house called Strawberry Field. John used to slip through the fence and play for hours in the woods that surrounded it.

STRAWBERRY
FIELD

AUNT MIMI'S HOUSE
251 Menlove Avenue

JOHN'S
ROOM

FRONT PORCH
where Aunt Mimi made
John practise the guitar so
she couldn't hear him.

The guitar is all
very well, John, but
you'll never make a
living at it!

Mimi wanted John to work hard at school, but his reports said he was hopeless, acted like a clown in class, and was on the road to failure. All John wanted to do was play the guitar his mother had given him. As a teenager he saw quite a lot of his mother, and it was a terrible shock when she was killed in a road accident.

Not far away, in a little house on Forthlin Road, lived Paul with his father, mother and brother Mike.

THE McCARTNEYS
20 Forthlin Road

BLUE
SUBURBAN
SKY

FRONT ROOM
where John and Paul later
wrote over 100 songs

His voice just isn't
good enough!

Paul did well at school. He enjoyed singing, though he was turned down when he applied to join the cathedral choir. When he was fifteen his mother died. Paul had just been given a guitar. He lost interest in school and spent all his time playing it.

Around this time skiffle music was popular in England. Skiffle was simple to play. You needed a guitar or a banjo, but the other instruments could be made at home. This was important, as few kids then could afford to buy instruments.

## INSTRUMENTS FOR A SKIFFLE GROUP

**WASHBOARDS and THIMBLES**
The thimbles clattered out a rhythm on a washboard (every house once had one, for rubbing clothes clean).

**TEA CHEST BASS**
made from the large boxes used for shipping tea, a broom handle and a piece of string.

**GUITAR or BANJO**

## TEDDY BOY OUTFIT
fashionable at the time

ducktail hairstyle

string bow tie

long drape jacket

tight drainpipe trousers

pointed winklepicker shoes

Also just becoming popular was American Rock 'n' Roll. As well as Elvis Presley and Buddy Holly, John and Paul were mad about black singers like Little Richard and Chuck Berry.

ELVIS PRESLEY & BUDDY HOLLY

LITTLE RICHARD & CHUCK BERRY

John's school was called Quarrybank. He started a skiffle group called *The Quarrymen* with some friends. One hot day in 1956 they played at the St Peter's Church fete. A friend of John's brought Paul along to watch.

Wow! he makes up his own words!

He's a genius. he can play the guitar upside down!

When John couldn't remember the words, he invented his own. Paul thought this was very clever. He showed John some new chords on the guitar. Being left-handed, Paul turned the guitar round and played it upside down. John was so impressed he asked Paul to join the group.

Paul had been making up songs since he first got his guitar, and soon John was writing songs too. Whenever Paul's dad was out, they would spend their time practising at Paul's house. Then one day Paul introduced John to George, who was in the year below him at school.

This is George.

He's just a kid.

But he knows a lot of chords.

His hair's very long!

THE HARRISONS
25 Upton Green, Speke

George, your hair needs cutting!

Oh no, Dad! Not those blunt scissors again. They hurt!

George was the youngest of four. To save money his father used to cut the children's hair at home, which George hated. His mother got him a guitar and encouraged him to play. He practised hard. John and Paul asked George to join them because he knew a lot more chords than they did.

The group was starting to become quite popular locally. By now John had left school and gone to Art College, where he asked his friend Stu to join them. Stu bought a bass guitar. He used to stand with his back to the audience so nobody could see he didn't know how to play it.

STU     JOHN     PAUL     PETE     GEORGE

When the group were invited to go and play in Hamburg in Germany, they asked another friend, Pete, to join them as drummer. Since John had left Quarrybank School, they'd changed their name several times. They finally decided on The Beatles because they wanted an insect name like Buddy Holly's Crickets, but they spelt beetles with an 'a' because they played music with a strong beat.

In Hamburg the Beatles were often on stage for eight hours a day. It was hard work but very good practice, and they got better and better. They were even asked to play on a record called 'My Bonnie'. Then Stu met a girl called Astrid who suggested that they all brush their hair forward in what would become the famous Beatle-style moptop. Only Pete kept his hair greased back.

When the others returned to Liverpool Stu decided to stay in Hamburg with Astrid. Now there were only four Beatles. Paul took over on bass guitar and they began playing regularly at a club called The Cavern. Whenever they played, people queued all down the street to get in.

One day three different customers went into a Liverpool record shop and asked for 'My Bonnie'. The manager, Brian Epstein, had never heard of it, but he soon discovered that the Beatles were playing just round the corner at The Cavern.

So one lunchtime he went to see what the fuss was about. He was at least ten years older than anybody else in The Cavern and felt rather out of place. The Beatles looked scruffy and dirty to him, but even so he thought they were fantastic.

A few weeks later Brian Epstein arranged to meet the Beatles in his office. Paul was late because he'd been at home having a bath. That annoyed Brian, but even so he said he would like to become the Beatles' manager.

Brian worked hard to organise the Beatles, smartening them up and arranging lots of performances. Next he went to London to see the record companies. None of them thought the Beatles were good enough. Then a record producer called George Martin listened to the recordings Brian had brought. 'Very interesting,' he said.

A month later the Beatles went to London to play live for George Martin at the Abbey Road recording studios. 'Very nice,' said George Martin – but they still had to wait another two months before he made up his mind to make a record with them. And he didn't think Pete the drummer was good enough. When the Beatles finally went back to Abbey Road, they had a new drummer – Ringo.

John, Paul and George had known Ringo for a while because he was the drummer with another top Liverpool group. Ringo was brought up by his mum in a tiny house near the city centre. He'd been a sickly child and first started playing the drums in hospital. His real name was Richard Starkey, and his nickname Ringo came from all the rings he wore.

MRS STARKEY'S HOUSE
10 Admiral Grove

We'll start recording now. Let me know if you don't like anything.

Well, for a start, I don't like your tie!

Love me do...

The first song George Martin recorded with the Beatles was 'Love Me Do', which reached number 17 in the charts. Their next song, 'Please Please Me', got to number one. They were on tour with a singer called Helen Shapiro at the time. Helen was meant to be the star but the audiences began going crazy for the Beatles, and by the end of the tour they were getting far more applause than she was.

The Beatles' third record, 'She Loves You', went straight to number one. When word got out that they were appearing on a TV show at the London Palladium, fans kept arriving all day.

Soon there were thousands outside, screaming so loud that nobody inside could hear to rehearse. Suddenly the Beatles were the biggest news in Britain. They were even asked to appear at the Royal Variety Show a few weeks later, in front of the Queen Mother.

The show was seen on TV by a fantastic 26 million people. The world was about to experience *Beatlemania*. Nothing like it had ever been seen before, and nothing quite like it has been seen since.

Wherever the Beatles went, huge crowds appeared. Soon people in other countries heard about them. When they went to France thousands of fans came to London Airport and begged them not to leave.

When their fourth record 'I Want to Hold Your Hand' went to number one in the USA, the Beatles flew to New York to appear on the famous Ed Sullivan show on TV. Ten thousand teenagers greeted them at the airport. Hardly any crimes took place during the show because everybody was watching, including the criminals!

Later, at a party at the British Embassy, some very posh people got carried away and began fighting for autographs. Some of them even produced scissors and tried to snip pieces from the Beatles' hair as souvenirs.

For three years, Beatlemania raged. It's hard now to imagine what it was like. You can get some idea by seeing a film about the Beatles called *A Hard Day's Night*, which was made in 1964.

Paul!

George!

John!

Ringo!

All I want for Christmas is a Beatle . . .

People made up songs about the Beatles. Shops everywhere sold Beatle souvenirs. There were Beatle dolls, Beatle wigs, boots, dresses, sheets, pillowcases . . .

BE A HIT! in this BEATLE WIG!

FAB! **BEATLE BOOTS**

GENUINE *BEATLES' HAIR*

ACTUALLY contains a lock of hair from one of the Fab Four.

GEAR!

REAL LEATHER

Everything the Beatles said was reported in the newspapers. Every time a Beatle record came out it went straight to number 1. Everywhere they played there was so much screaming they could hardly be heard.

When George said he liked jelly babies, audiences began pelting the stage with them. British jelly babies are soft. In America there are only jellybeans, which are hard and hurt!

Can you imagine what it was like –
never to be left alone for a minute,
always in a plane, a hotel room or a
huge stadium? The Beatles felt trapped.
So in 1966 they gave up performing.
Instead, they went into the studio to
record 'Sergeant Pepper's Lonely Hearts
Club Band'. It was full of new sounds,
such as tapes played backwards and
Indian instruments. It changed pop
music for ever.

Since so many people had heard their songs, the Beatles had begun to think
they should use them to say something important. When they appeared on
the first TV show that linked the whole world by satellite, an audience of 400
million saw them sing 'All You Need is Love'. At the time American soldiers
were fighting a war in Vietnam. A growing number of people thought this was
wrong, and the Beatles' message of love and peace exactly caught this mood.

John and Paul had soon been recognised as exceptional songwriters. They wrote hundreds of songs. The more they wrote, the better they got. It's interesting how they came up with ideas.

## YESTERDAY

Paul woke up one day with the tune for his most famous song playing in his head. It sounded so good that he imagined he must have heard it somewhere. For ages he couldn't think of any words, so he called it 'Scrambled Eggs'. Then he thought of 'Yesterday', which fitted perfectly with the rather sad tune.

## LUCY IN THE SKY WITH DIAMONDS

One day John's four-year-old son Julian came home with a painting he'd done of a girl at school called Lucy, who he said was 'in the sky with diamonds'. John was reminded of Alice 'in a boat on the river' in *Through the Looking Glass* – a favourite book. This dreamlike song was the result.

Some of the best Beatles songs are about childhood memories of Liverpool.

SHELTER in middle of ROUNDABOUT

BANK

BARBER SHOP

### PENNY LANE
Paul wrote this about a local shopping street he and John both knew well. The places mentioned in the song are still there.

Yellow matter custard, green slop pie, all mixed together with a dead dog's eye.

### I AM THE WALRUS
John took some of the words for this from a playground rhyme which Liverpool boys used to sing to upset the girls

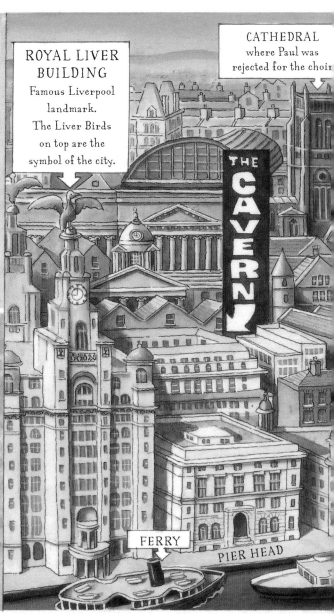

ROYAL LIVER BUILDING
Famous Liverpool landmark. The Liver Birds on top are the symbol of the city.

CATHEDRAL where Paul was rejected for the choir

THE CAVERN

FERRY

PIER HEAD

You can still see many of the places they sang about.

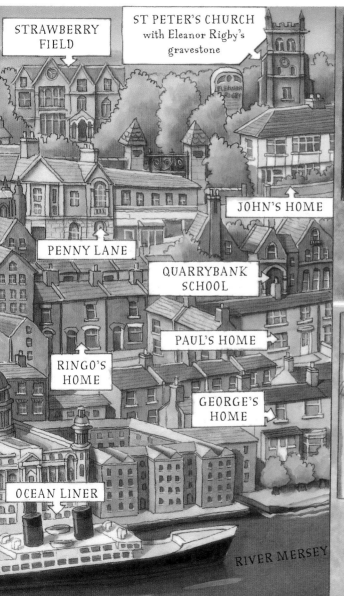

STRAWBERRY FIELD

ST PETER'S CHURCH
with Eleanor Rigby's
gravestone

JOHN'S HOME

PENNY LANE

QUARRYBANK
SCHOOL

PAUL'S HOME

RINGO'S
HOME

GEORGE'S
HOME

OCEAN LINER

RIVER MERSEY

This is where
I used to play.

### STRAWBERRY FIELD
This was the orphanage near Aunt Mimi's
house with the woods where John used to
play when he wanted to be alone.

That's amazing!
I was sure I made it up.

### ELEANOR RIGBY
Paul thought he had invented the name
Eleanor Rigby until someone noticed
it on an old gravestone in the same
churchyard where he first met John.

All four had begun to look for more in life than just being Beatles. An Indian guru (a teacher) known as the Maharishi taught them to spend time each day in quiet thought. They were with the Maharishi when they heard some terrible news. Brian Epstein was dead, after accidentally taking too many sleeping pills. They had relied on him to organise everything for them.

BRIAN EPSTEIN

That year brought another shock for the Beatles. A film they made called *The Magical Mystery Tour*, about them going on a bus trip with some friends, was not a success. Up to that point everybody had loved everything they did, but now Beatlemania was over. They were still hugely popular, however, and a cartoon based on Paul's song 'Yellow Submarine' was a big hit.

The Beatles were drifting apart. They had all got married and were following their own interests. Even so they made two more terrific albums. The first, 'Abbey Road', has the famous cover which shows them on the pedestrian crossing outside the studios where they recorded all their songs. Tourists still come from all over the world to be photographed on the same spot.

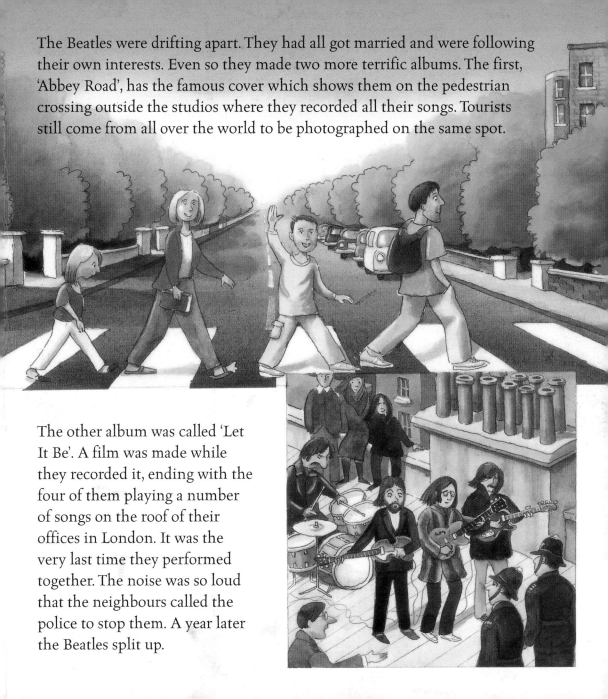

The other album was called 'Let It Be'. A film was made while they recorded it, ending with the four of them playing a number of songs on the roof of their offices in London. It was the very last time they performed together. The noise was so loud that the neighbours called the police to stop them. A year later the Beatles split up.

**John** went on to write many unforgettable songs and campaigned for peace with his wife Yoko. The world was shocked when a crazy fan murdered him in New York in 1980.

**George** proved that he too could write memorable songs, and was very successful on his own. He died from cancer in 2002.

**Paul** started a new band, Wings, which was hugely successful. He wrote many more hit songs. In 1997 the Queen made him Sir Paul.

**Ringo** made several records and films but is perhaps best known today as the voice of Thomas the Tank Engine.

The Beatles have been copied by so many bands that it's hard to realise how new and different they once seemed. But their songs are played constantly, and still make people feel good.